THE OFFICE OF
President

BY JAMES McCAGUE

GARRARD PUBLISHING COMPANY
CHAMPAIGN, ILLINOIS

Library of Congress Cataloging in Publication Data

McCague, James.
    The office of President.

    SUMMARY: A survey of the United States Presidency with
a discussion of the influence of eight particular men on
the office.
    1. Presidents—United States—Juvenile literature.
[1. Presidents] I. Title.
JK517.M33   353.03'13   75-9937
ISBN 0-8116-6510-0

Picture credits:

The Bettmann Archive: pp. 15, 50, 69 (all)

Brown Brothers: pp. 11, 22, 27 (top), 44, 65, 77

The John Carter Brown Library, Brown University: p. 4

Imperial War Museum: p. 66

Library of Congress: pp. 33, 36

The Metropolitan Museum of Art, Gift of Col. and Mrs. Edgar
    William Garbisch, 1963: p. 19

Pinkerton's, Inc., New York: p. 47

Franklin D. Roosevelt Library: p. 80

Underwood and Underwood, New York: pp. 56, 59

United Press International: pp. 39, 76, 79, 85, 90
    (middle and bottom right), 93 (top)

Wide World Photos: pp. 90 (top and bottom left), 93 (bottom)

Cover painting by Victor Mays

Contents

"A Display of the United States of America,"
engraved in honor of the new Constitution and
the nation's first president.

1. A Government Is Born

The American War is over, but this is far from the case with the American Revolution.

Dr. Benjamin Rush
(written in 1783)

For nearly four months, delegates from twelve states had been meeting at the Pennsylvania State House in Philadelphia. They had argued and talked among themselves. Slowly and patiently they had settled most of their differences. Now at last, on September 17, 1787, the work of the Constitutional Convention was finished.

One after another, 39 delegates rose, walked to the center of the hall, and signed their names to the Constitution of the United States.

Not all the delegates were satisfied with it, however. A few refused to sign. One state, Rhode Island, had not even sent any delegates to the convention. The new Constitution still had to be approved, also, by special conventions in at least two-thirds of the thirteen states in order to become law. But, as one delegate said, those who signed felt that this Constitution was the best one they could all agree on.

The Constitution set up three separate branches of government. A Congress, consisting of a Senate and a House of Representatives, was given the sole power to make laws. A Supreme Court, together with lower courts, would decide all disputes that arose from the laws. A president was made head of the government. Seeing that the laws were enforced would be his most important duty.

It had been hard for the delegates to agree on this office of president. Some had realized that no president could be a good leader if they limited his powers too much. Others, though, had been fearful that the office might become too powerful.

In its final draft, the Constitution simply told how the president was to be elected, gave the oath of office he must take, and made him commander in chief of the nation's army and navy. It also said that he must be a natural-born citizen at least 35 years old, and that he must have lived in the United States at least 14 years at the time of his election.

The president was given the right to

appoint certain other government officials, but only with the "advice and consent" of the Senate. He could also make treaties with other countries, but the treaties then had to be approved by at least two-thirds of the Senate. In addition, he might veto any act passed by Congress. His veto could be set aside, however, by a two-thirds vote of both the House of Representatives and the Senate.

All this left some doubts about other powers of the president. It left many people wondering, too, just what kind of a leader their president was likely to be. Americans in the 1700s tended to think of any national leader as a sort of king. Thus many of the delegates themselves thought the president should be given such elegant titles as "His Mightiness,"

"His Highness," or "His Elective Majesty."
Even after the Constitutional Convention
ended, many people were not sure what
had been accomplished.

The story goes that a Philadelphia lady
went up to Benjamin Franklin, who had
been a delegate from Pennsylvania.
"Well, doctor, what have we got," she
asked, "a republic or a monarchy?"

The wise old statesman answered simply: "A republic—if you can keep it."

2. A President Takes Charge

There is a rank due to the United States among nations which will be withheld, if not absolutely denied, by the reputation of weakness.

George Washington

Cannons roared from the decks of warships anchored in New York harbor. Again and again they fired, booming out a solemn thirteen-gun salute. Sailors high in the rigging cheered and waved their hats as a long, graceful boat glided across the water from the New Jersey shore. The boat's twelve oars moved in perfect time, rowed by harbor pilots dressed in spotless white. On the prow of

One artist's version of the glorious arrival of George Washington to New York.

the boat was a beautiful figurehead of Columbia, spirit of the United States. Under a red, white, and blue canopy at the stern stood George Washington, with high government officials around him.

Amid more cheers from crowds on shore, the boat pulled up to a dock at the foot of Wall Street. Washington went ashore. Then he climbed into a waiting carriage and was driven to a house on nearby Cherry Street. Thus the first president-elect of the United States arrived at his executive mansion. New York City was the nation's temporary capital at this time.

The date was April 23, 1789, a week before Washington's inauguration. During those seven days, no doubt, he did some serious thinking about the problems he faced. The president had been chosen by a unanimous vote of the nation's electors. Americans everywhere loved and respected him for his heroic leadership in their war for independence. Nevertheless, shortly before setting out for New York, he had written to a friend that he foresaw "a sea of difficulties" ahead.

Government by the people still was a new and untested idea. New Hampshire had ratified the Constitution just ten months earlier. It was the ninth state to do so, which made the necessary two-thirds of the thirteen. History was going to be made during the next few years. How it was made—whether well or badly —would depend very largely on President George Washington.

He began his term in office with great care, resolved to obey the Constitution in every way. Yet he knew he could not rely on the Constitution alone. It said nothing about a president's advisers, for example. So Washington promptly appointed a cabinet, as presidents have done ever since. Thomas Jefferson of Virginia was secretary of state; Alexander Hamilton of New York was secretary of the treasury. For secretary of war, the president decided on Henry Knox of Massachusetts. Edmund Randolph, another Virginian, was asked to be the attorney general.

The four made a well-balanced group. Hamilton and Knox were leaders of the Federalist party, which stood for a strong central government. Washington himself leaned toward the Federalists, though he was not a party member. Both Jefferson and Randolph were Democratic Republicans. This was the group which

The first cabinet meets. From left to right: Henry Knox, Thomas Jefferson, Edmund Randolph, Alexander Hamilton, and President Washington.

later became known as the Democratic party. Its members believed in curbing the federal government's power in favor of states' rights and individual liberty.

George Washington's chief concern was to make the country strong. To help accomplish this goal, Alexander Hamilton was given the task of setting up a sound system of money and credit. Hamilton proposed that the federal government take over all debts left from the War of Independence, including all of the states' debts. Congress soon passed the necessary laws and the president signed them. Federal bonds were issued to cover the debts. Then part of the money taken in taxes each year was set aside to pay off the bonds. In this way the young nation began to build confidence among its own people and those of other countries also.

Next, Hamilton urged Congress to create a national Bank of the United States, which would provide a standard form of money everywhere in the country. It would be run by private bankers but controlled by federal officials. Many lawmakers said that such a bank would make the federal government far too strong. Besides, these men claimed, the Constitution gave Congress no power to create a bank. Hamilton answered that power did not have to be stated in so many words. It was *implied*, he said, because it was part of the Congress's power to levy taxes and to regulate commerce.

He convinced the Congress. President Washington signed the bank's charter in 1791.

This first statement of the doctrine of

implied powers was important. It meant that future presidents and lawmakers could interpret the Constitution so as to meet the needs of a growing, changing nation.

Washington believed that a president should hold himself above political quarrels. Throughout his first term he managed to do so. After his reelection in 1792, however, a war between England and France caused some bitter arguments among Americans. The Democratic Republicans wanted to enter the war on France's side. When the president declared that the United States would be neutral, taking neither side, they raised a storm of protest. But Washington's decision stood, for he was on firm ground. Though the Constitution gave Congress the sole right to declare war, it contained no rules about neutrality. Washington felt free, therefore, to take this responsibility upon himself.

In 1794 a tax on whiskey caused more trouble. Whiskey makers in western Pennsylvania rose in revolt and refused to pay the tax. The president's answer was that government by the people would be impossible unless laws were

President Washington reviews the troops used to put down the Whiskey Rebellion.

obeyed. He sent soldiers out against the rebels, and they gave up without firing a shot. In the end, this so-called Whiskey Rebellion became a test of the government's right to make and enforce laws. Thanks to Washington's swift, stern action, that right was never in doubt again.

George Washington refused to accept a third term as president. His farewell address was printed in a Philadelphia newspaper, but it was never given in the form of a speech. In it he urged all Americans to put loyalty to the nation above their loyalty to any state or political party. And he went on to say: " 'Tis our true policy to steer clear of permanent alliances with any portion of the foreign world."

Those words would guide the nation for more than a hundred years to come.

3. A President Makes a Purchase

Laws and institutions must go hand in hand with the progress of the human mind.

Thomas Jefferson

Along the Potomac River the new federal city of Washington was taking shape. Great stretches of it were still swampland. The main street, Pennsylvania Avenue, was a muddy dirt road. Not even the national Capitol on Jenkins Hill was finished. Only its north wing, where the Senate met, was ready for business. There, at noon on March 4, 1801, Thomas Jefferson took his oath of

Thomas Jefferson's inauguration was a simple affair. The third president is seen here as he arrived alone at the Capitol.

office as third president of the United States.

It was the first inauguration to be held in Washington, D.C.

Federalist John Adams, who followed George Washington, had had a stormy four-year term. A bloody revolution in France had set the countries of Europe to fighting among themselves. This in turn had caused great unrest in the United States. The Federalists, trying to put down the unrest, had passed a series of laws called the Alien and Sedition Acts. Among other things, the acts made it a crime to find fault with Congress or the president. Worse still, Federalist officials enforced the acts as harshly as they could. By 1800 most Americans had had enough. They voted the Federalists out and the Democratic Republicans in.

The young nation had passed its first great test. Perhaps Benjamin Franklin had foreseen something like this back in 1787 when he said that the government was "a republic—if you can keep it."

In his inaugural address Thomas Jefferson pleaded for friendship between the two political parties. He promised to be a wise and thrifty president. Then he went quietly back to his boardinghouse for dinner—and found that nobody had saved a place for him at the table.

In its own small way, that incident showed how different Jefferson was from the first two presidents.

George Washington always had made a point of the great dignity of the presidency. So had John Adams. Both men had surrounded themselves with servants in fancy uniforms. Every affair of state had been stiff, solemn, and sedate. But Jefferson cared nothing about ceremony. The British ambassador was shocked when he called at the White House one day and the president met him in "yarn stockings and slippers down at the heel."

Jefferson believed that the country would get along best with the least amount of government. Under him the Alien and Sedition Acts were speedily repealed. So were several tax laws. To make up for the lost taxes, Jefferson did away with many federal jobs created by the Federalists. He also reduced the size of the army and navy.

Thomas Jefferson's greatest feat as president was the purchase of Louisiana. His object at first was simply to keep the Mississippi River open to American commerce. In those days, the great river was the only practical way for Americans in frontier regions west of the Allegheny Mountains to send their goods and crops to market. They used flatboats which floated down the Ohio and Mississippi rivers to New Orleans at the Mississippi's mouth. The cargoes were either sold there or loaded aboard oceangoing ships and sent off to other markets still farther away.

Any hostile nation holding New Orleans could easily shut off this route, however. For many years Spain had owned the city as a part of the vast Louisiana Territory that stretched from the west bank of the Mississippi to the Rocky Mountains. Then came word that Spain had promised to give Louisiana to France in a secret treaty signed in 1800.

This was bad news. Americans had not been very happy about Spanish control of New Orleans, but French control worried them far more. Napoleon Bonaparte, the French emperor, was a warlike and ambitious man. No one knew what he might want to do.

Then, in 1802, just before France was to take possession of Louisiana, Spain

Thomas Jefferson more than doubled the size of the United States in 1803 with his purchase of Louisiana.

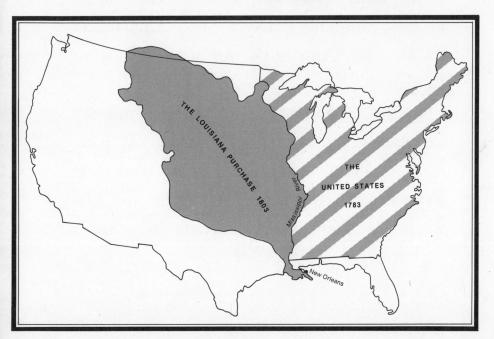

THE LOUISIANA PURCHASE 1803

Mississippi River

THE UNITED STATES 1783

New Orleans

closed New Orleans to river traffic. Americans were worried that the French, too, would interfere with their shipping.

President Jefferson acted quickly. He sent a delegation to Paris with an offer to buy New Orleans. First, though, he took care to ask Congress for permission. Congress not only gave it, but voted to let him pay as much as two million dollars for the city.

The meetings in Paris began. After some talk, France's minister of foreign affairs suddenly asked the Americans: "What will you give for the *whole* of Louisiana?"

Robert Livingston, of the American delegation, was hard of hearing. It took him a little while to understand the Frenchman's question. When he did, he made an offer at once. There was some bargaining; then both sides agreed to a price of about fifteen million dollars.

Now Thomas Jefferson had a hard decision to make. He had always believed that a president had no powers except those given him by the Constitution. Since the Constitution said nothing about buying new territory for the nation, he did not think he had any right to do it. He thought of asking Congress to pass an amendment to the Constitution which would give him the right. There was no time to lose, however, for Napoleon Bonaparte might change his mind.

Finally Jefferson did what he had to do. He directed the American delegation to sign a treaty that would give the Louisiana Territory to the United States. Then he told Congress that he had made the purchase.

Some members of Congress were not at all pleased. A senator from New Hampshire asked angrily: "If the president can purchase new states without the consent of the old, what is to prevent him from selling an old state without its consent?"

Most of the senators, though, approved the purchase and ratified the treaty with France on October 20, 1803. Thus, at one stroke and at a bargain price, the United States became more than twice as big as it had been before.

When it counted, Thomas Jefferson had the courage and the wisdom to put his country's good above his own ideas about the limited powers of the president. And in doing so he took those powers a long step forward for other presidents who would follow him.

4. A President of All the People

One man with courage makes a majority.

Andrew Jackson

People in Washington never had seen an inauguration day like this one in 1829 —and they never would again. So many visitors had flocked into town for it that they had slept four or five in every bed. The streets were jammed with people. After the inaugural ceremony an unruly crowd burst into the White House and gobbled all the food set out for the invited guests. Fist fights broke out as men pushed and shoved one another. Noses were bloodied, eyes blackened, furniture smashed. Several friends had to help the new president escape through a back door.

That was how Andrew Jackson took office as the nation's seventh president.

"The reign of King Mob seemed triumphant," declared one man who was there. Another was sure that the country was ruined.

Both gentlemen failed to realize that times were changing, and so was the United States. In the nation's early years, only men who owned property had been allowed to vote. Many thousands of people had had no voice in electing presidents. All the while, though, a strong, active middle class was growing in numbers and in strength. Most states slowly

A cartoonlike painting of Andrew Jackson's inaugural party. The president's guests are depicted here as an unruly mob.

did away with their old voting laws. Now many middle class men could vote, and in Andrew Jackson they had chosen a new kind of president.

Four of the first six men to hold the office—Washington, Jefferson, James Madison, and James Monroe—were well-to-do Virginia landowners. The other two, John Adams and his son John Quincy Adams, were members of a great Boston family.

But Jackson came to Washington from the frontier state of Tennessee. He had been a backwoods lawyer and judge. He had won fame as a general by defeating the British at the battle of New Orleans in 1815. His soldiers had given him a nickname that stuck: Old Hickory. He was a man of the people, and the people loved him for it.

Jackson's Democratic party had developed from the old Democratic Republican party of Thomas Jefferson. But Jackson did not share Jefferson's views on limited presidential powers. Unlike members of Congress, who were chosen by their own states or districts, the president was elected by the country as a whole. Therefore, said Jackson, it was his duty to guard the people's liberties "against the Senate, or the House of Representatives, or both together."

Those were fighting words, and he meant them. During his eight years in office, Andrew Jackson vetoed more bills than any president before him.

One veto put an end to the Bank of the United States. Over the years since the time of Alexander Hamilton the bank had grown great and powerful. Jackson

KING ANDREW THE FIRST.

This newspaper cartoon pictured Andrew Jackson as a tyrant trampling on the Constitution.

charged, however, that its wealthy stock-holders were prospering at the expense of all the citizens. In 1832 he vetoed a bill that would have renewed the bank's charter.

Many of the country's biggest business-men were staunch friends of the men who ran the Bank of the United States. They raged against Andrew Jackson. He was called a tyrant. Newspaper cartoons showed him wearing a crown and trampling on the Constitution as "King Andrew the First."

Nevertheless, Congress failed to pass the rechartering bill over his veto. And on election day, later that year, the people had their say. They elected Andrew Jackson to a second term.

Old Hickory showed his fighting spirit again on the touchy question of states' rights.

The trouble began with tariff laws passed by Congress in 1828 and 1832. Southerners claimed that the laws favored northern businessmen. People in South Carolina objected most bitterly of all. Their state legislature finally passed an Ordinance of Nullification. This was a resolution saying that the tariff was "not binding upon this state, its officers, or citizens." Many politicians of the time believed that a state had the right to nullify, or set aside, any federal law its people disliked.

The president did not agree. "Nullification means insurrection and war!" he said. He asked Congress for a law giving him the right to use national troops in South Carolina. He had already stationed these troops nearby. He threatened to have the state's leaders arrested and tried for treason. If they were found guilty, said Jackson, he would see that they were hanged.

It was no bluff. Everyone knew that Andrew Jackson would do just what he said he would. Then Congress hastily passed a more favorable tariff bill and the president signed it. The leaders

Jackson fought South Carolina's decision to set aside federal law. He was determined to preserve the Union at any cost.

of South Carolina thus had a chance to back down gracefully.

The president had made his position clear. He stood for the Union, first and last.

"I do precisely what I think just and right," Andrew Jackson once said. He did indeed; yet with all his toughness and strength of character, he was a man of action rather than a thinking man. And his actions did not always work out quite the way he expected. In doing away with the Bank of the United States, he upset the nation's entire system of money and credit, and years of hard times followed.

Jackson could be a hard man too. His Indian policies were cruel and unjust. On one occasion he even ignored a verdict of the Supreme Court in order to drive the friendly Cherokee Indians from their land.

Throughout his two terms, nevertheless, Old Hickory kept most of his fellow Americans on his side. He understood the American people. He knew what they were thinking, how they felt, what they expected of their government.

Because this was true, Andrew Jackson made the presidency an expression of the people's will more surely and deeply than it ever had been before.

5. A President Stands Fast

*We must settle this question now —
whether in a free government the
minority have the right to break it up
whenever they choose.*

Abraham Lincoln

Hours dragged by. It was almost ten
o'clock on a Sunday night, and weary
members of the House of Representatives
wanted to go home. But Congressman
Benjamin Stanton of Ohio was determined to bring his Force Bill to a vote.
The bill would give the president the
power to call volunteer soldiers from all
the states to serve with the United
States Army.

These were troubled times. A Virginia congressman had already warned that if the bill passed, his state would leave the Union.

"It must pass this evening," Stanton had answered.

But it did not pass, for another man rose and moved that the House adjourn. The motion was seconded and passed. The 36th Congress of the United States went out of existence, and with it went the Force Bill.

The next day, Monday, March 4, 1861, the nation's sixteenth president was inaugurated. He was a homely small-town lawyer from Illinois named Abraham Lincoln. His Republican party was a new one, only seven years old, and he took office in a land divided by angry threats of war.

The bitter old question of states' rights over the power of the national government never had been settled. Since Andrew Jackson's presidency, disputes over slavery had kept the bitterness growing on both sides. The Northern states had done away with slavery. Northern people thought that the South should do so too. But Southern leaders felt that they had the right to own slaves regardless of the Northern point of view. Tempers had grown hotter as the disputes went on. By election time in 1860, Southerners were declaring that they would not accept a Northern Republican as president.

Lincoln's victory was more than they could bear.

Before the end of 1860, South Carolina seceded, or withdrew, from the Union.

Mississippi, Florida, Alabama, Georgia, Louisiana, and Texas soon followed. Leaders of these seven states prepared to organize a new nation, called the Confederate States of America. They announced that they were ready to go to war to keep their independence.

What to do about this split in the Union became Abe Lincoln's problem on his first day in the White House.

President Lincoln called up volunteers, even though the Constitution did not clearly give him the right to do so.

Some men thought there still was a chance that the leaders of the seceding states would change their minds. So for a month the new president did nothing to upset the uneasy peace. Long afterward, in a letter to a friend, he wrote: "I claim not to have controlled events, but confess plainly that events have controlled me."

Then on the night of April 12, 1861 came the event that ended all hope of peace. Confederate soldiers fired on the Union's Fort Sumter in Charleston harbor, South Carolina.

The president at once issued a call to the states for 75,000 volunteer soldiers. His right to do this was far from clear, for Congress never had passed the Force Bill. Virginia, Arkansas, Tennessee, and North Carolina protested by joining the seceding states. But Lincoln was resolved to put down the rebellion. He told Salmon P. Chase, his secretary of the treasury:

"These rebels are violating the Constitution to destroy the Union; I will violate the Constitution, if necessary, to save the Union; and I suspect, Chase, that our Constitution is going to have a rough time of it before we get done with this row."

Now the country was caught up in a civil war. Perhaps the president did not realize at first how bloody and terrible the war would be, but he knew that winning it would require bold leadership.

For four long years he never shirked his bitter task.

Calling up volunteers was only a very small first step. Before long, men were being drafted into the army by force. Soon Lincoln suspended the right of

The Civil War president interpreted his powers as commander in chief broadly. He is seen here on the battlefield at Antietam.

habeas corpus, an age-old rule of law which protected people from being put in jail without fair trials. Anyone suspected of favoring the Confederate States could then be thrown into federal prisons and kept there on any pretext—and hundreds of innocent people were.

As the war went on, Lincoln spent huge sums of federal money without the consent of anyone in the government, though Congress alone was supposed to have that right.

Congress grumbled and argued, but it went along. The Constitution and the people's liberties were indeed having "a rough time of it." The United States mails were barred to all letters suspected of containing disloyal ideas. Some newspapers that disagreed with the government's policies were forced to close.

Many people grew angry about all this. For a long time the war went badly for the Union. That made people angry too. Lincoln's political enemies—and he had plenty of them—heaped abuse on him. He was called "the original gorilla," because of his homely face and his tall, lanky frame. Some people made fun of his slipshod, careless ways, such as his filing of important papers in the tall stovepipe hat he wore. His habit of telling funny stories annoyed others.

Underneath these outward appearances, though, Abe Lincoln was one of the most intelligent politicians of his time, or of any time. His determination was as strong as iron. Like Andrew Jackson 30 years before him, he understood his fellow Americans and had faith in their good sense. Perhaps that was what he

Victorious Union troops marching in Washington
at the close of the Civil War.

meant when he said, during the war's darkest days:

"For my own part, I consider the first necessity . . . is of proving that popular government is not an absurdity."

In the end that *was* proved. The war was won, and the Union was saved. Then, shortly after the Confederates' surrender, an embittered southern actor murdered Abraham Lincoln. Thus he became our nation's first martyred president.

Abe Lincoln's five years in the White House had been hard, tragic years. In his role as commander in chief, he had stretched the powers of the office farther than any other president ever had dared to do. Only a truly great man could have done that while still preserving government by the people.

6. A President with a Big Stick

*Speak softly and carry a big stick and
you will go far.*

Theodore Roosevelt

Jolting and swaying on the steep
mountain road, a carriage plunged on
through the night. It was pitch-black; the
road was rough and dangerous. Yet each
time the driver tried to slow down his
horses, his passenger ordered calmly:
"Push on!"

The passenger was Theodore Roosevelt,
vice-president of the United States. Word
had just reached his hunting camp in

the Adirondack Mountains that President William McKinley had been shot by an assassin at Buffalo, New York, and was dying.

On September 14, 1901, as the nation mourned McKinley, Theodore Roosevelt took his oath of office and became the 26th president.

Roosevelt, who was only 43, was a new kind of Republican politician. He had been a boxer in college. He had written a history book. He had run a western ranch. He was a hunter and mountain climber. He had fought in the recent Spanish-American War at the head of his own volunteer cavalry troop, the Rough Riders. Though born to wealth himself, he had made his start in politics by speaking out against those he called "the wealthy criminal class."

The nation was going through a time of great unrest. Years of vast and speedy growth had followed the Civil War. They had been prosperous years too—well named the Gilded Age. Not everybody had shared in the prosperity, however. Rich businessmen had grown richer while poor men and women worked long, hard hours for low pay. Now people were impatient for a change.

New political parties—the Populists, the Progressives, the Socialists—were demanding laws to stop the evils of the Gilded Age. Everyone was eager to see what the new president would do.

Roosevelt soon showed them.

First he acted to break up the groups of giant corporations known as trusts. The directors of these trusts were used to running American business as they pleased. They ignored laws and bribed lawmakers, stole public lands, and piled up huge profits for themselves. Many people thought the trusts could never be destroyed. But Roosevelt acted swiftly.

The coal trust, railroad trusts, food trusts—all were taken into court. The government won its first case. Then the great financier J. Pierpont Morgan, one of the country's most powerful men, called at the White House. Morgan was an officer in many of the biggest trusts. Perhaps a compromise could be worked out, he suggested.

"There can be no compromise in the enforcement of the law," answered the president.

The trust-busting, as it was called, went on.

Under Roosevelt's strong leadership,

On a tour of the West in 1903, Roosevelt drummed up support among the people for his far-reaching programs.

other reforms came quickly. Laws governing fair play in business were made stronger. New standards of cleanliness and purity in food and drugs were set. Because Theodore Roosevelt loved the out-of-doors, he was one of the first presidents to realize the importance of saving our woods and streams and wild animals. He set aside millions of acres, to be held by the government as a public trust.

These reforms, which we take for granted today, were new ideas in those early years of the 1900s. Many people were shocked and startled by them. But Roosevelt was far too strong a leader to be discouraged by opposition.

Theodore Roosevelt had very simple ideas about the president's powers. He believed he could do anything unless the Constitution actually forbade it, and he often stretched his powers to the limit. At least once he went a little past the limit. That was how work got started on the Panama Canal.

People had talked about the canal for a long time. But the Central American country of Colombia refused to sell the rights to the necessary strip of land to the United States. Finally Roosevelt lost patience. He encouraged a small band of Colombian rebels to create their own independent country, named the Republic of Panama. In return they sold the United States the right to use a portion of their land for the canal.

Congress was unhappy about this meddling in another nation's affairs. Members threatened to hold up approval of the treaty with Panama. That bothered the president not one bit.

Roosevelt inspects the building of the Panama
Canal from inside a giant steam shovel.

"I took the Canal Zone and let Congress debate," he boasted, "and while the debate goes on, the canal does also."

In 1907 Roosevelt decided to send the United States Navy's main battle fleet around the world. He wanted to impress other countries with our increasing strength as a world power. But Congress objected. Several senators reminded the

president that they could stop him by re-
fusing to vote any special money for the
trip.

Very well, said Roosevelt. The navy already had enough money on hand to send
the fleet halfway around the world. He,
as commander in chief, certainly had the
right to order it put to sea. Then if
Congress chose to leave the ships
stranded on the other side of the world,
Congress could explain to the American
people!

He had his way. Sixteen United States
battleships steamed around the world,
and the world was duly impressed with
the nation's strength.

In his private life, as in his public one,
Theodore Roosevelt was always a man of
action. Throughout his two terms there
seldom was a dull day at the White

House. Callers were likely to find him romping on the lawn with his six children, boxing with some famous prizefighter, or lecturing to a visiting Boy Scout troop. When he left office in 1909, he said:

"No president has ever enjoyed himself as much as I have enjoyed myself. . . ."

He undoubtedly meant it. But his years in the White House added up to more than a good time. Theodore Roosevelt was a bold and vigorous president, who matched the vigorous new 20th century. This was doubly important because a succession of presidents, for some 30 years past, had let the powers of the office become steadily weaker.

Roosevelt had changed that. In his hands the presidency had come to mean strong leadership once more.

7. A President Goes to Europe

The interests of all nations are our own also. We are partners with the rest.

Woodrow Wilson

Whistles blew. Church bells rang. All over the United States happy people celebrated. It was November 11, 1918, and World War I had just ended in Europe.

At the White House in Washington, President Woodrow Wilson and his advisers were planning their next move. The United States had helped England, France, and Italy to defeat Germany in the war. Now Wilson was determined to help create a just and lasting peace.

Early in December he sailed for France to meet with leaders of the other nations and decide on a peace treaty.

No president before Wilson ever had gone to a foreign country during his term in office. But Woodrow Wilson already had proved that he was not bound by old habits or ideas. A Democrat, he had been elected president in 1912 and re-elected in 1916. He had promised to give the country strong new laws, and he did.

High tariffs were lowered, thus encouraging foreign trade. The first income tax law was passed. This law spread the cost of government more fairly among the people. Wilson's Federal Reserve System brought badly needed government control to the nation's money and banking.

When war broke out in Europe, Wilson tried to keep this country neutral. But when the United States finally entered the war in 1917, he proved to be a wise and able leader.

Long before Germany was defeated, the president had begun to look ahead and think about peace. He first described his famous Fourteen Points in a speech to Congress in January 1918. Together, these points told of Woodrow Wilson's ideals for worldwide justice and goodwill.

Several of them provided that no nation should seize any lands belonging to her neighbors. Other points forbade secret treaties between nations and bound all large countries to reduce the size of their armies and navies. Still others dealt with fair and sensible policies toward colonies all over the world. The fourteenth

President Wilson leaves for the Versailles Peace Conference.

point provided for a League of Nations. The league would settle disputes between countries and protect the rights of all.

The people of Europe gave President Wilson a hero's welcome. Everywhere he went he was hailed as the man who had saved democracy. Then the leaders of the so-called "Big Four" nations—England, France, Italy, and the United States—

The signing of the peace treaty at Versailles.
Woodrow Wilson is seated fifth from left.

met in the Palace of Versailles, close to Paris, to write the peace treaty.

Trouble soon started there. Most European statesmen cared nothing about Wilson's Fourteen Points. Each man thought only of selfish advantages for his own country. Many of their countries already had secret treaties with each other, and they meant to keep them. Some were greedy for Germany's former colonies. All were determined to punish Germany for starting the war.

Woodrow Wilson fought hard for his ideals. One by one, however, he had to give up his points or agree to compromises that badly weakened them. Only on point fourteen did he refuse to compromise. When the Treaty of Versailles was written at last, it included the provision for a League of Nations.

To Wilson the league was all important. He sailed for home in July 1919 to submit the treaty to the Senate. Now he faced another fight. Republicans held control of the Senate, and they had their doubts about the Versailles treaty. One small, stubborn group of senators, called isolationists, were against all foreign ties. Another group, led by Senator Henry Cabot Lodge of Massachusetts, was willing to approve the treaty only if the League of Nations was not included. They felt that the league should be considered later, by itself.

Here President Wilson made a bad mistake. He had compromised with the European leaders, but he would not compromise with Henry Cabot Lodge. Instead he made up his mind to take the matter directly to the American people.

SAFELY THROUGH THE FOG AND STORM—BUT NOW THE
DANGEROUS RAPIDS TO SHOOT!
From *Central Press Association* (Cleveland)

COAST TO COAST
From the *World* (New York)

Newspaper cartoons of
the day described the
pitched battle between
Senate and president
over the peace treaty.

LOOKING A GIFT HORSE IN THE MOUTH
From the *Beacon* (Wichita, Kansas)

On a special railroad train, Wilson traveled thousands of miles through western and midwestern states. He made long, stormy speeches in city after city. But most Americans wanted only to forget World War I and the problems it had caused. The idea of a League of Nations meant little to them.

Woodrow Wilson finally wore himself out in the losing fight. He suffered a stroke, and then another, which left him partly paralyzed. For months he lay helpless in the White House, cut off from the outside world.

Meanwhile, the Senate refused to ratify the Treaty of Versailles.

A Republican, Warren G. Harding, won the presidency in 1920. Congress passed a resolution ending the war, and Harding signed it. The last hope of the United

States joining the League of Nations was gone. Americans busied themselves with their own affairs. They turned away from the rest of the world and its problems.

In 1924 Woodrow Wilson died, a tragic man almost forgotten by his countrymen.

Yet in time Wilson would be remembered as a president who had given the office a strong voice in foreign affairs.

His high ideals and his belief in his nation's destiny had not been in vain either. The United States was too big, too powerful to turn away from the rest of the world. Wilson had seen that very clearly.

Few people realized that in the 1920s. A time was coming, though, when the United States would take its place as a leader among nations. Some Americans would remember then that Woodrow Wilson first showed the way.

8. A President Becomes a World Leader

It is common sense to take a method and try it. If it fails, admit it frankly and try another.

Franklin D. Roosevelt

In the fall of 1929 hard times hit the United States. Businesses all over the nation began to fail. Factories shut down; millions of people were out of work. Banks closed, and people lost their savings. Farmers, unable to sell the crops they raised, were driven off their land. Bewildered men and women everywhere asked each other what could have gone wrong.

The nation had seemed prosperous throughout the 1920s. Three Republican presidents had followed Woodrow Wilson. First was Warren G. Harding; then Calvin Coolidge; then Herbert Hoover. Under them, after the troubled times of World War I, had come growth and rapid change. Businesses had thrived. Factories turned out more and more goods of every kind. Not everyone had shared in the prosperity, however.

Wages paid to many working people had lagged behind the high profits made by businessmen. The prices of farm crops had been low also. As a result, millions of workers and farmers lacked the money to buy the nation's manufactured goods. In addition, new high tariff laws passed in 1921 and 1929 cut down our foreign trade. So factories became idle.

These things and more finally caused the Great Depression. Few people understood why it came about. Everywhere they looked, Americans saw only hungry people, deserted factories, and empty stores. By 1932 an angry, worried nation had had enough.

The Democratic candidate, Franklin Delano Roosevelt, promised the voters a New Deal. They swept him into the White House by a landslide.

Huddled around their radio sets, people listened to the new president's inaugural address. They liked what they heard. "The only thing we have to fear is fear itself," Roosevelt declared. He himself was a good example of courage, for he had been stricken by infantile paralysis many years before. He had to get about in a wheelchair, and he could stand up only with the aid of clumsy, uncomfortable leg braces. But his illness had never beaten him. People liked that too.

The new president was a distant cousin of Theodore Roosevelt. With all the first Roosevelt's vigor and self-confidence, he got his New Deal moving.

Congress was called into a special session and presented with a steady stream of bills from the White House. Each was a bold new idea never before tried in the United States. The senators and congressmen quickly enacted them into law.

Few of these ideas were Franklin D. Roosevelt's own. Although he had great personal charm and political skill, he was a man of action rather than a deep thinker. But his advisers, known as the "Brain Trust," were people of many different backgrounds. Among them were

An army of unemployed was put to work—

college professors, politicians, businessmen, and labor leaders. Frances Perkins,
whom Roosevelt chose as his secretary of
labor, was the first woman ever to hold
a cabinet post. These people worked out
the president's New Deal laws.

Some of the laws helped farmers. Some
set up controls over business. Others put
thousands of jobless people to work
building roads, dams, and national parks.

in programs like the Civilian Conservation Corps.

The Social Security Act of 1935, the greatest forward step of all, launched a broad new program of federal unemployment and old-age insurance for American workers.

As time went on Roosevelt did not always manage to get along with Congress. And several New Deal laws were declared unconstitutional by the Supreme Court. Yet in spite of such setbacks the president was still the hero of a vast majority of Americans. Toward the end of his second term, many Democratic party leaders urged him to run again.

No president ever had tried for a third term. But now World War II had begun in Europe. One country after another was being crushed by Adolf Hitler's German armies. Across the Pacific in Asia, Japan had attacked China. More and more, it appeared that the United States would be drawn into the fight for world freedom.

In that spirit Franklin D. Roosevelt ran for a third term and won.

Little more than a year later, Japan's sneak attack on Pearl Harbor, Hawaii, brought the war home to all Americans.

"We are in it—all the way!" Roosevelt told his stunned nation. "Every single man, woman, and child is a partner in the most tremendous undertaking of our history."

As always, his leadership inspired the people. Night and day shifts in American factories turned out the guns, tanks, ships, and airplanes needed by free nations fighting for their lives. Over sixteen million Americans fought on land and sea

December 8, 1941: Franklin Roosevelt condemns the bombing of Pearl Harbor and asks Congress for a declaration of war.

In meetings with Winston Churchill (left) and Joseph Stalin (right), Roosevelt became a world leader.

around the world—and nearly half a million of them died—before the war was won at last.

Roosevelt was more than president of the United States now; he was a world leader too. Working closely with Winston Churchill, England's great prime minister, and with Premier Joseph Stalin of Russia, he helped direct the course of the war everywhere. The three leaders, and their advisers, also planned the peace settlements that would follow the war's end.

One of the things they agreed on was a world organization called the United Nations. This organization would be very much like the old League of Nations for which Woodrow Wilson had fought so hard.

World War II ended with the surrender of Japan in September of 1945. Unfortunately, President Roosevelt did not live to see it. Unwilling to leave his job till it was done, he had run for a fourth term in 1944. Again he had won. But the burdens he had carried so long finally proved too heavy. He died on April 12, 1945.

Franklin D. Roosevelt was president for more than twelve years. (No man will ever serve so long again. In 1951 the

22nd Amendment to the Constitution limited all presidents to two terms.)

Through those stormy years Roosevelt led his country and his people into a new era of vast change and progress. Part of that change concerned the presidency itself. With Franklin D. Roosevelt, it became the single most powerful office in all the world.

Along with the power went hard new problems too—as future presidents would find.

9. A President Resigns

*We need a national government that
is the servant and not the master of
the people.*

Gerald R. Ford

On a July morning in 1974, Richard M.
Nixon, the 37th president of the United
States, sat alone in the study of his home
at San Clemente, California. Grimly he
waited for news from far-off Washington.
The news, when it came, would mean
either victory or defeat in the hardest
battle of Richard Nixon's life.

The crisis was not his alone. Many
Americans believed that the future of the

presidency itself was at stake. Thus it was the nation's crisis too.

Ever since Franklin D. Roosevelt, the United States presidency had grown more and more powerful. Harry S. Truman, who succeeded Roosevelt, had been followed by General Dwight D. Eisenhower, popular hero of World War II. John F. Kennedy, elected to office in 1960, had shown great promise of world leadership until his tragic murder three years later. Then Lyndon B. Johnson had stepped in and proved to be another strong, able president.

Throughout this period of more than 20 years, the Congress had been content to let presidents do very much as they thought best. Finally, with Richard Nixon, presidential power had reached its peak.

President Nixon's achievements in foreign affairs were most impressive. He managed to pull American troops out of a long, costly war in Southeast Asia which had troubled Americans for many years. Nixon also traveled to Peking, China, and to Moscow, the capital of the Soviet Union. Both nations had been bitter rivals of the United States ever since

President Nixon and Chou En-lai shake hands in a historic breakthrough in foreign affairs.

World War II. In face-to-face talks with their leaders, the president made a hopeful start toward building world peace and goodwill.

At home Nixon promised a stable and efficient government.

In November 1972, he was elected to a second term by one of the greatest landslides in American history. Though he was a Republican and the Democrats held control of Congress, the president's popular support seemed strong enough to overcome all opposition.

Then his troubles began.

During that 1972 campaign a group of men hired by Nixon's reelection committee broke into Democratic party headquarters in a Washington, D.C., building called Watergate. They had planned to spy on Democratic campaign leaders. They were caught, however, and the trial was set for January 1973, two months after the election.

Hardly anyone paid any attention at first, in spite of newspaper stories linking the Watergate burglars with men in the White House. The incident had little or no effect on the election. But after the men were found guilty and sent to jail, stories about the break-in continued to raise serious questions.

As more and more evidence piled up, a Senate committee was appointed to look into the Watergate affair. Then one of the men in jail talked. He claimed that he and the others had been promised money in return for not telling about the Nixon men who had hired them. The con- victed burglars were called before the Senate committee as witnesses. As the scandal began to grow, the attorney general appointed a special prosecutor to find out whether any others had committed crimes.

Soon the committee found evidence that top members of Nixon's White House staff were involved in plots to punish and discredit the president's political enemies. Some had tried to misuse federal agencies to that end. Others had apparently broken the law in raising money for the president's reelection. The committee also found out that Nixon had had secret tapes made of all his conversations with his top aides.

Most of the president's men were forced out of their jobs at the White House. Eventually, many were accused of various crimes by the special prosecutor, tried, and sent to prison.

In a separate case about this time, Vice-President Spiro Agnew was accused of accepting bribes and cheating on his income taxes. He resigned under fire. The president appointed Gerald R. Ford, a respected congressman from Michigan, as the new vice-president. Meanwhile, the Watergate scandal kept growing.

Presently there was talk of impeaching the president. The Judiciary Committee of the House of Representatives began to investigate whether there were grounds for impeachment. Still, President Nixon denied that he had known what was going on. Certain of the secret tapes contained important evidence, or so it seemed. Yet the president refused to permit either the special prosecutor or the Judiciary Committee to hear these tapes on the grounds of executive privilege.

THE WATERGATE STORY

The president's men testify.

The Judiciary Committee considers impeachment.

The tapes are delivered to the court.

The people wait.

This principle, first stated by Thomas Jefferson, held that a president need not furnish evidence to any court if he felt it might be harmful to the country. Over the years the principle had often been argued, but never finally settled.

This time, though, the question was finally taken all the way to the United States Supreme Court. And on that July morning at San Clemente, the president received news of the Supreme Court's decision.

He had lost. The Court ordered him to turn the tapes over to the special prosecutor.

Nixon knew that one of the tapes would prove that he had ordered his aides to cover up their parts in the Watergate break-in. His impeachment by the House of Representatives on a charge of obstructing justice was now almost certain. He knew that too. Shortly after returning to Washington, he learned of other charges against him. He also learned that most of his supporters in the Senate, where he would have to go on trial, could no longer stand by him.

On August 9, 1974, President Nixon resigned. The same day Gerald Ford was inaugurated as the nation's 38th president.

For nearly two years Watergate had troubled and vexed all Americans. It had split them into angry groups, for and against the president. Many thoughtful people had feared that the country could not survive a long and difficult impeachment trial. Many others felt that the Congress had grown weak during the long years of growing presidential power. They doubted that congressmen and

On the historic morning
of August 9, 1974, the
president resigns under
fire, and a new president,
Gerald Ford, is sworn
into office.

senators would dare to take any action against the president.

Yet in the end the American system of government worked. The law, as set forth in the Constitution, still ruled the land. The Congress found the courage to face up to its duty.

Great and strong as the presidency had become, it was not a power unto itself. Nor did it depend on what happened to any man. Though both Nixon and Agnew had resigned, Gerald Ford—not elected but only appointed to the vice-presidency —was able to take office without a single voice raised in opposition.

Once again, as old Ben Franklin would have said, the people kept their republic.

Index